Thousand-Year Whispers

Thousand-Year Whispers

Rona Laycock

Graffiti Books

Thousand-Year Whispers
Rona Laycock

Published by Graffiti Books 2022
Malvern, Worcestershire, United Kingdom
Email: graffitibooksuk@gmail.com
Website: www.graffitibooks.uk

Graffiti Books is the book publishing arm of *Graffiti Magazine*

Printed and bound by Aspect Design
89 Newtown Road, Malvern, Worcs. WR14 1PD
United Kingdom
Tel: 01684 561567
E-mail: allan@aspect-design.net
Website: www.aspect-design.net

All Rights Reserved.

Copyright © 2022 Rona Laycock

Rona Laycock has asserted her moral right
to be identified as the author of this work.

The right of Rona Laycock to be identified as the author
of this work has been asserted in accordance with
Section 77 of the Copyright, Designs and Patents Act 1988.

This book is sold subject to the condition that it shall not, by
way of trade or otherwise, be lent, resold, hired out or otherwise
circulated without the publisher's prior consent in any form
of binding or cover other than that in which it is published
and without a similar condition including this condition being
imposed on the subsequent purchaser.

Front cover photograph Copyright © 2022 Rona Laycock
Cover Design Copyright © 2022 Aspect Design

ISBN 978-1-9163339-4-9

For David

Make me this present then: your hand in mine,
and we'll live out our lives in it.

(Michael Donaghy)

Contents

Acknowledgements	ix	From the Journal	36
About the Writer	xi	Maidenhair Tree	38
Thousand-Year Whispers	1	Western Red Cedar	39
The Journal	3	Box Elder	40
In the Beginning	5	From the Journal	41
Cedar of Lebanon	9	Bhutan Pine	44
Katsura	10	Juniper	45
Douglas Fir	11	From the Journal	47
From the Journal	12	Wire Netting Bush	52
Wollemi Pine	14	Incense Cedar	53
Yew, the Tree of Death	15	Seven Son Flower	54
From the Journal	16	Serbian Spruce	55
Persian Ironwood	17	Dawn Redwood	56
Spindle	18	From the Journal	58
Swamp Cypress	19	Monkey Puzzle	60
From the Journal	20	Common Beech	61
Sapphire Dragon Tree	24	Holly	63
Ash	25	European Larch	64
From the Journal	26	From the Journal	65
Giant Sequoia	28	Western Hemlock	67
Bladdernut	29	Scots Pine	68
Erman's Birch	30	Shagbark Hickory	70
From the Journal	31	Prickly Myrtle	71
Oriental Plane	33	From the Journal	72
Paperbark Maple	34	To the NHS & others	72
Indian Cedar	35	Sweet Chestnut	74

Angelica	75	Strawberry Tree	87
Atlas Cedar	76	From the Journal	88
Roble Beech	77	Lawson Cypress	89
From the Journal	78	Holford Pine	90
Bishop Pine	79	Handkerchief Tree	91
Kyushu Lime	80	Furin-tsutsuji	94
Amur Maackia	81	Broad Leaf Lilac	95
From the Journal	82	Indian Bean Tree	96
Service Tree	84	Great White Cherry	97
Snowdrop Tree	85	Postscript	99
Japanese Cedar	86	Bibliography	101

Acknowledgements

I am grateful to so many people who have inspired, encouraged and supported me throughout life. I taught creative writing for many years and learnt far more from my students than they learnt from me. As they are too many to name I will just say that if you attended one of my courses – thank you.

From the bottom of my heart I thank Catchword writing group members – Liz Carew, Martin Wilkinson, Derek Healy, Gill Garrett, Pam Keevil, Jan Turk Petrie, Meg Berry-Davis, Pam Orr, Susannah White, all talented writers.

The late Welsh poet, Nigel Jenkins, introduced me to the haibun and I feel the need to thank him, posthumously, for opening a door into a world I did not know existed.

This book is dedicated to my husband, David, who has been my best friend ever since we first met and who patiently read and re-read this book during its development – that's real love for you!

About the Writer

Rona was born in North Wales and arrived in the Cotswolds in the late eighties via Tunisia, Pakistan, Egypt and Ireland. Each place she has lived, worked and travelled in has inspired and informed her writing and there are many wisps of her poetry and prose scattered around the world that will testify to that.

Her first poetry collection, Borderlands, was published in the form of an audio CD and reflected on her experiences in some of those far flung places.

She started her working life as a school teacher but over the years had to turn her hand to play many different roles whilst living abroad. Returning to the UK she worked for NGOs where she found herself running emergency management and response projects amongst other things.

Eventually she found her way back to teaching and enjoyed a very fulfilling career teaching creative writing in colleges and arts centres.

During this time she achieved both an MA and PhD from Swansea University – an experience that was challenging and thoroughly enjoyable.

She likes to inhabit the border between poetry and prose when she writes and this makes the haibun a favoured form.

Thousand-Year Whispers

What stories these trees would tell us if they could speak.

> the wind in the trees
> leaf to leaf and bough to bough
> thousand year whispers

In 2019 my husband, David, and I joined the team of volunteers at the National Arboretum, Westonbirt, Gloucestershire but our training was put on hold when Covid-19 hit the country. It is in no small part due to the enthusiasm and encouragement of the trainers and other volunteers that we persevered.

Being able to walk through the trees with a purpose during that stressful time helped to keep our spirits up. The more we learned the more we realised just how little we knew of the trees that are all around us and that give us shelter, pleasure and, indeed, life.

There is a two-thousand year old coppiced lime tree in the arboretum. A living thing that can trace its lineage back to a time when druids were worshipping in oak groves, Boudicca was queen of the Iceni and the Romans were busy building roads across its new colony, Britain – imagine that.

This book is not a botanical reference book. It is meant to be something you can dip into now and again to read some of the wonderful facts, stories and myths that surround us every day when we visit trees. Woven between the trees are pages from a sporadic journal I kept during 2020 and 2021 – the Plague Years! These excerpts are an attempt to capture those experiences and their physical and emotional impact on our lives.

I hope you enjoy reading it and that it will encourage you to further explore our amazing natural world.

The Journal

We arrived at 2020 with the usual anticipation that this is the year we will do this or learn that; no one predicted we would have little chance of achieving anything other than learning to live in isolation. When the coronavirus, now known as Covid-19, first arrived we had no idea that this tiny object would bring such illness, mental health issues, relationship problems, death and the promise of economic ruin to a world unprepared for something that, in hindsight, seemed inevitable.

From the start I decided to keep a record of our experience and it seemed natural to do this in the form of haiku and haibun. These Japanese forms are ideal for travelogues and also for diary entries and I am grateful to the late Welsh poet, Nigel Jenkins, for introducing me to them and for his encouragement during the years he supervised my PhD in Swansea. These forms lend themselves to combining the public and personal experience as well as trying to find light relief in these strange times. I have taken liberties with the form, of course, in the same way that I have played fast and loose with chronology.

How future generations will view these years is a mystery to those of us living through them but I would like to leave a small contribution to the mountain of literature that will no doubt emerge from the experience.

In the Beginning

On 11 March 2020 the World Health Organisation declared Covid-19 a pandemic.

After some time listening to news of this new virus and with no clear advice from the government we have decided to take our own measures. We are suffering coughs and colds but no temperature so we think we do not have the illness but we keep our distance from others just in case we spread whatever it is to people who are more vulnerable.

> first day of Lockdown
> I keep thinking that we now
> face a silent world

We have been working on our new way of life – when and where to shop for food, which of us will shop each time and what to buy. How strange that the first things to sell out in the shops are toilet paper and tinned tomatoes. I'd like to see what sold out in other countries – that could be the basis of a PhD thesis looking at cultural differences in times of crisis.

Our much looked forward to holiday in Beaumaris in April has to be postponed. We have changed the date to the end of October, I wonder if things will be better by then. We have cancelled our trip to Cape Cod for our nephew Daniel and his fiancée Tracey's wedding, so disappointing for us but more so for them as they have had to postpone it.

Life is changing and we will experience several 'firsts', good, bad and indifferent.

> end of the first day
> the sky darkens, now we face
> the first Lockdown night

We live in a small village in Gloucestershire and it did not take long for people to anticipate what might be needed during the pandemic. Neighbourhood groups were set up and contacts were publicised to ensure help is always available for shopping, picking up medication, keeping us up to date on the latest advice or simply a friendly voice on the phone or on the village street. A reassuring resource at a time when we are wondering how things will turn out.

There is also something reassuring about the way nature reclaims a space we no longer occupy. I have often thought that humans are like a virus with too many of us using too many resources and everything else on Earth suffers. Well, here we are. A virus has laid us low and nature is moving in – wild goats coming down from the Great Orme to explore the streets of Llandudno, fallow deer browsing on a housing estate in East London and increased sightings of otters, orca and other aquatic mammals.

The weather has been amazingly unseasonal, with bright sunshine and higher than normal temperatures. It won't last, of course, but each day brings us closer to summer. The dawn chorus is ramping up the volume as the birds find mates, build their nests and prepare for their young.

> the robin answers
> the blackbird's dawn call
> I wake too early.

> blackbird, wren, robin
> they are not interested
> in why our world changed

We have had bird boxes by our back door for years and they are visited sporadically. The newer one is the chosen dwelling this year and a couple of blue tits have been inspecting it each day but it appears they have company.

       solitary bee
       explores the bird box causing
       the blue tits alarm

Cedar of Lebanon
(*Cedrus libani*)

Lebanon, once called the Pearl of the Mediterranean, is now a wrecked country. Years of unrest, political corruption and, more recently, a massive explosion have left it battered but, perhaps, not bowed.

Once home to the Phoenicians, invaded and ruled by the Romans, a leading centre of Christianity and then conquered by Arab Muslims, it is hard to imagine a more magnificent and complex history.

If you thought deforestation was a new phenomenon, read the *Epic of Gilgamesh*. Written approximately four thousand years ago, it tells the story of Gilgamesh, ruler of Uruk, opening up the vast forests of the Eastern Mediterranean to humanity. Since those days the Cedar of Lebanon was mentioned in the Bible as being used to build the Temple of Solomon. It was used in Egyptian sarcophagi, Phoenician ship building and, in the First World War, what was left of the cedars was chopped down as fuel for steam trains and as sleepers to support the rails. It is classified as 'vulnerable' in its own homeland. The last remaining old growth groves of the Cedar of Lebanon are on the high slopes of Mount Lebanon in the Cedars of God World Heritage Site.

It flies proudly on the flag of Lebanon today and has been adopted by us to adorn our parks and country estates. What a tragedy it would be if future generations could not enjoy its iconic appearance in its own homeland.

> Basho-like wisdom
> 'learn of cedars from cedars'
> time is all it takes

Katsura
(*Cercidiphyllum japonicum*)

We are beginning to appreciate the different scents trees give off. For several days in autumn the smell of toffee apples or candyfloss wafted through some of the glades in the arboretum and we tracked the source to a tree called the katsura. It is particularly beautiful in the autumn when its leaves change from green to yellow, pink, peach and orange. The sugary smell is strongest then, as the leaves fall, although some people seem to be unable to detect the scent – and they assure me they can smell other things so they are not suffering from Covid-19!

So many trees seem to leave their best until autumn. As if they keep those last bursts of glory until just before they shut down for the winter.

>enjoy falling leaves
>another year is turning
>we can start again

Douglas Fir
(*Pseudotsuga menziesii*)

Named after the wrong man? Apparently David Douglas recorded the nature and potential of the trees but it was Archibald Menzies who first documented their presence on Vancouver Island in 1791, eight years before Douglas was born. Menzies gets a mention in the botanical name of the tree but Douglas has the lion's share of the publicity!

Just to add to the story – the Douglas fir is not a true fir, but belongs to a different sub-family of pines.

> pine needle tea
> another gift from the trees
> just choose carefully

The cones have tridentine bracts that peek out from under the scales looking for all the world like the tail and back legs of tiny mice. I learnt a new word – exserted – it means to cause to protrude and is the term to describe these bracts.

I have read the North American First Nation's mythology that goes along with these cones which describes mice as hiding in them or that they were trapped in there by a Douglas fir that was fed up with them stealing all the seeds. Apparently it is the first tree that children in British Columbia learn to identify.

> wide eyed as a child
> I visit your old stories
> wondering what next

From the Journal

Time has slowed and normal weekly chores are put off for another day which is fine in principle, the trouble comes when they are outside chores and the weather decides not to cooperate. Forgetting the vagaries of our weather my mind turns to the idea of time and how it passes differently depending on your age. I remember interminable maths lessons, rainy days that were definitely longer than the sunny ones and the way the six-week school summer holiday was gone in a flash.

I have a couple of favourite quotes regarding time. One from Douglas Adams, 'Time is an illusion, lunchtime doubly so' and another from the excellent *Old Harry's Game* written and performed by Andy Hamilton on Radio 4, 'Time is what stops everything happening all at once'.

> after days of sun
> the fragrance of rain.
> Petrichor, I think.
>
> the rain is needed
> spring showers to freshen us
> but we miss the sun

During the past few weeks we have been watching a live feed from a webcam that is placed near an osprey nest in North Wales. The Glaslyn ospreys have produced three chicks and we have thoroughly enjoyed seeing them grow. There have been dramas, rogue ospreys overhead, crows and peregrines harassing the parents and the worry that the youngest chick is not being fed as much as the others. Unjustified fears; the mother knows exactly what she is doing.

There is quite a history of these birds in Wales: they turn up in the Mabinogion, feature on the coats of arms of both Swansea and West Glamorgan and a Welsh rugby union team is known as the Ospreys.

Glaslyn is not far from Porthmadog and the volunteers that run the centre have done a great job engaging the public with their live online streaming.

These beautiful birds winter in Africa and return to their nest on the Glaslyn estuary each spring. They are a welcome sight. It is extraordinary to learn that they were once hunted by egg and skin hunters years ago; people who emptied the skies of ospreys.

> Welsh Gweilch y pysgod
> heraldic ospreys fly high
> to return to us

Around 9 July 2020 the oldest chick, KC2, fledged. She flew around a little and sat on the branch that sticks out from their nest. She still cuddles in with her siblings when it rains and at night, so it seems she will not be leaving home any time soon.

Wollemi Pine
(*Wollemia nobilis*)

How can it be that a tree thought to have been extinct for millions of years is found alive and well in 1994 only 150 km from the city of Sydney, Australia? Perhaps others had passed through the canyon where David Noble found them but did not give them the attention needed. He stopped long enough to see the strange bubbly bark that resembles Coco Pops and the unusual leaves. A lesson to us all to pay attention to the world around us.

I like the fact that because it appears to have risen from the dead it is described as a living fossil or a Lazarus taxon!

>thought to only live in stone
>*Wollemia nobilis*
>returns to the world

These trees are so precious to the Australians they have their own fire-fighting battalion to protect them during bush fires. They have become emblematic of the value of wilderness areas and have been celebrated in poetry and song since their discovery.

You can buy and plant your own wollemi but there are only around 100 surviving in the wild and they are under threat from a fungal pathogen thought to have been introduced into the canyon by unauthorised visitors.

>time to stop and think
>walking in, walking out
>you could bring death

Yew, the Tree of Death
(*Taxus baccata*)

Death and sorrow – ancient Egyptians stirred up those connections by using the foliage to symbolise mourning. The Romans used the wood on their funeral pyres and still today stories that send shivers down your spine surround these dark green trees.

Take the Llangernyw Yew growing in a village churchyard in North Wales. A truly ancient tree, thought to be four thousand years old, whose cleft trunk is said to be a portal to the land of the dead and which is visited annually by the Angelystor – 'Recording Angel'. Apparently, each Halloween the angel whispers the names of parishioners who will die before the next Halloween. As with many such stories there is a disbeliever who spends the night in the church after wagering that there is nothing to the tale. The next day his hair has turned white and he refused to say whose name he heard being called. He died before the next Halloween.

The yew is poisonous, every part of it . . . apart from the soft red berry-like flesh that surrounds the toxic seed. Birds eat these with impunity but it is not for the likes of us. The interesting thing is, the toxins in the yew have been synthesised and used as effective treatments for certain types of cancer. The way trees and other plants contain chemicals that we can use as medication makes me anxious that the loss of so many trees around the world means we might never know what benefits they have for us until they are almost extinct.

> standing in sunlight
> it becomes its own shadow
> that ancient yew tree

From the Journal

We have never been enthusiastic gardeners; we like to see the garden looking reasonably tidy but also like the fact that unkempt gardens attract more wildlife.

The front garden was reorganised a few years ago and has a selection of very pretty trees and shrubs.

>flowers fading fast
>*Magnolia stellata*
>petals fall like snow

The first week of this new restricted life I decided to clean all the cupboards in the kitchen and found several forgotten, unused items. Once charity shops open again we will take them along as donations and someone else can make good use of them. The money raised will be much needed to make up for the lack of income during these months. The jars that were out of date had to be investigated and most were still okay and could be used. I suspect I am not alone in deciding to spend a bit of time reorganising or sorting through kitchen cupboards during Lockdown!

>basil, chervil, seeds
>found in a cleaned out cupboard
>now planted in hope

Persian Ironwood
(*Parrotia persica*)

A tree after my own heart. When winter comes and other trees shut up shop, the Persian ironwood decides to flower! Tiny but abundant red flowers develop on its bare branches.

I also love the fact that it is named after a Mr Parrot, more correctly Herr Friedrich Wilhelm Parrot, who 'botanized in the Alborz on a mountaineering expedition in the 1830s' according to Wikipedia!

The leaves in autumn shine out red, orange, yellow and purple – another reason the epithet Parrot seems apt.

>sunshine in the glade
>a hundred Persian colours
>hide silver-green bark

Spindle
(*Euonymus europaeus*)

It's called spindle because its hard dense wood was used to make spindles for spinning wool. It is also used to make knitting needles. A cosy domesticated tree that also provides food for hundreds of insects and birds but, and there is always a but, the leaves and fruit are toxic to us humans. The most benign form of that toxicity is as a laxative but if enough berries are eaten it can cause unconsciousness, kidney failure and even death. Perhaps the *Sleeping Beauty* story had its origins in this tree.

Some call it the 'Burning Bush' because its autumn foliage is so dramatic. Its flowers are pink and can be seen in May and June. They develop into bright pink fruits containing orange seeds. In some places it is said that if the flowers appear earlier than usual an outbreak of plague is coming. I wonder when they flowered in 2020!

>cobwebs on spindles
>those gossamer threads are too fine
>to veil your colours

Swamp Cypress
(*Taxodium distichum*)

These trees are used to sharing their environment with alligators in places like the Everglades but, once upon a time, they lived near Bournemouth. Okay, a little poetic licence is being used here. The swamp cypress trees were living in that part of the world before Bournemouth was a place, traces of their fossils are found on the Jurassic Coast.

The tree was reintroduced in 1640 by a character called John Tradescant the Younger, gardener to Charles the First, no less. He voyaged to Virginia three times, apparently taking with him a musket and armour as protection from the indigenous people who objected to these Europeans coming along and taking their resources without permission. I suspect some of his travelling companions might have been carrying smallpox, measles and other diseases to a fresh New World that had no immunity to such viruses. The spread of the Covid-19 virus we are experiencing today is an echo of that time.

The swamp cypress can develop 'knobbly knees' to help with stability and which can act like snorkels to help the tree breathe in waterlogged soils – according to information gleaned from the Royal Parks website.

The wood is used in making barrels and window frames because it is resistant to water – well it would be, wouldn't it?

>a tangle of trees
>taken from the Powhatan
>paid for with smallpox

From the Journal

In our garden we have watched birds nest, lay eggs, feed their young until they fledge and leave the nest. Spotting ducklings is a cause for celebration but we were worried that the strange loss of water a few weeks ago had damaged the fauna and flora of our precious stream but nature is nothing if not resilient and as the water returned so did the ducks. Not so sure about other species, though. We can but hope.

This year we have noticed so much; this anthropause, as it has been named, has given us the chance to slow down and observe our environment without other activities pressing on our time.

> the wind rattles leaves
> from somewhere on the river
> a duckling answers

> stop counting the days
> life is happening now –
> a wren feeds her chicks

It is all too easy to take things for granted when the world is 'normal' but when you are wrong-footed by circumstances you start to look for positives and our home is definitely that.

The stream at the bottom of the garden has returned to its more natural state after some strange happenings. The water all but ceased to flow for a while and then, when the flow resumed, the water turned white. Someone downstream took samples to try to find out what caused it. No doubt we shall hear in due course but for now we take pleasure in watching the wildlife that inhabits the stream.

> a small trout rises
> takes a fly in a second
> and silently sinks

We can't find the white clawed crayfish that used to be so numerous in previous years and hope they have not gone forever. On occasion we would find their bodies on rocks in the stream and wondered what was feasting on them, then one day we saw a moorhen killing one and then eating it. Moorhens are omnivorous. One destroyed our tomatoes in a particularly sneaky way by eating just the bottoms of the tomatoes. We had no idea until we picked them and found gaping holes in the underside of the fruits of our labours!

The stream needs some care now and again. We try to leave it alone as much as possible to allow the wildlife – flora as well as fauna – to do its own thing, but now and again we have to clear areas of rampant water mint and irises. Today was one of those days. An hour or so of pulling up the vigorous plants creates a nice little open space for herons and little egrets to land and take off and to afford us a view of aquatic insect life, a change from the garden ants that seem to have thrived these past few months.

> after clouds – the sun
> how do they know when to leave
> flying ants take wing

22

Pheasant

Heron

Peacock butterfly

'Feed me!'

Sapphire Dragon Tree
(*Paulownia kawakamii*)

That has to be one of the coolest names for a tree. Sapphires and dragons – it does not get much better. A *Lord of the Rings*–type saga with that title is just waiting to be written. The fact that in 1998 there were thought to be fewer than thirteen mature sapphire dragon trees left in the wilds of the Far East just adds to the idea of a quest to save them. Can you believe that wild populations of these trees were cleared to make room for orchards? Then again, food has to take priority sometimes.

It bears clusters of large violet flowers, reminiscent of foxgloves, which appear in early spring before the leaves.

> dragon in the woods
> gifting us violet gloves
> under the spring sky

Ash
(*Fraxinus excelsior*)

those black buds, flowers
in purple, green and yellow
lost to Chalara

There are some new words you don't want to learn but need to in order to understand just how life teeters on a knife edge. Chalara is such a word. Our ash trees are disappearing because of chalara, a fungus that attacks them and causes them to lose their leaves and crowns. At the time of writing, across the country, thousands of dead and dying ash trees are being felled to prevent them from falling across roads or causing damage.

What can be done? Research into resistant strains is going on but this catastrophe further underlines the need for biodiversity.

In Norse mythology the ash tree, Yggdrasil, was known as the World Tree. Its trunk reached into the heavens, its branches reached every country on Earth and its roots dwelt in the Underworld. Here in Britain, the tree was believed to have health-giving properties, particularly where children were concerned. New-borns were given a little of the sap and sick children were passed through a cleft of the branches in the hope they would be cured. Such a weight of legend will be lost with the trees when they are gone.

these dying ash trees
how the woodpeckers miss them
where will they drum now

From the Journal

There are times when we are not permitted to travel far from home, sometimes the limit is as little as five miles, and on those days we wander the garden looking, listening and discovering again just how lucky we are to have so much life around us. I hope we will continue to appreciate that when/if life becomes more normal. As the days pass one into the other during these strange times Haiku come unbidden to fill the pages when prose seems inadequate.

dandelion clocks
I will begin the countdown
with a silent breath

under the acer
cyclamen, periwinkles
brighten our Lockdown

leaf cutter bee
seen for the last time today
rain flooded her home

two blackbirds singing
'this is my territory'
hear, no love lost there

primroses abound
in the neglected garden
a lesson to us

        again and again
          bringing your yaffling laughter
            thank you woodpecker

            late sunlight – listen!
              sounds of the sea in the sky
                gulls so far inland

Night time brings its own sights and sounds and finds us outdoors watching the skies and hearing the nocturnal animals as they hunt for food or return to their roosts.

from east to west
   honking V-shapes split the clouds
   geese above the house

      through the darkened trees
        a trail scented by badgers
        followed by foxes

          one night in April
            waiting to spot satellites
            we see a vixen

            nocturnal surprise
              Space X Sky 'Train' not alone
              bats dance through the stars

                seen night after night
                meteor trails in the sky
                  they've travelled so far

                  hunting under stars
                    the owl, vixen and badger
                      break through the silence

Giant Sequoia
(*Sequoiadendron giganteum*)

There are several theories as to where the name 'Sequoia' comes from. My favourite is that it was named after Sequoyah, a Cherokee chief, who is credited with creating a Cherokee syllabary, thus allowing the Cherokee language to be written down and read.

These trees can grow to be the largest of all trees and the oldest living things on the Earth. The really big Sequoias have names – General Sherman, General Grant, Lincoln, Franklin, King Arthur, to name just a few. General Sherman is around 84 metres tall, around 31 metres in girth and estimated to weigh 21,000 tonnes.

A tree known as the Mother of the Forest was ancient and huge and, of course, somebody decided that it would be a good idea to remove a large section of its bark, ship it to New York, reassemble it and make a bit of money out of displaying it to the public as one of the 'vegetable wonders of the gold region'. Needless to say, the Mother of the Forest died.

> fallen Sequoia
> a wolf howls in harmony
> with her distant son

Their very fibrous bark and sap that is rich in tannic acid are said to protect them from fire damage in normal years. The year 2020 is terrible for forest fires in their native habitat, California; fierce fires that even these hardy trees might not survive. I wonder how many will be destroyed.

Bladdernut
(*Staphylea pinnata*)

These trees were new to me. Their seeds are held in papery bladders, hence the name. Although the botanical name, *Staphylea*, owes its existence to Pliny the Elder who, apparently, thought they looked like grapes and named it *Staphylodendron* – grape tree.

It often grows near streams and rivers and, when the time is right, it will drop the bladder-wrapped seeds into the water where they are carried away to germinate somewhere downstream. If you pop the bladders and look inside you will see that one of the chambers is empty, this acts as the floatation system. A simple yet ingenious device.

Apparently the seed can be eaten (this is not a recommendation on my part) and reportedly tastes a bit like pistachios. The seeds are sometimes polished and used to create rosaries.

> not content to stay
> even when fed and watered
> those seeds setting sail

Not a native but it was introduced into Britain around 1596 where gardeners chose it for its flowers and the seed bladders. I like the fact that when it is found growing wild in woodlands it is described as a 'garden escape'.

Erman's Birch
(*Betula ermanii*)

Beautiful bark, that's what caught my eye. Pink, cream and brown strips that shimmer when wet and give the tree a wonderful presence even when its leaves have dropped. In fact, winter helps it to show off its shape and colour. We are given the chance to see through the blowsy leaves to the elegance beneath.

> leaves stripped by the wind
> the nakedness of gold birch
> brings me more pleasure

Named for the physicist Georg Adolf Erman who spent 1828 to 1830 travelling around the world making magnetic observations. He obviously also observed nature and collected a specimen from its native habitat in Kamchatka.

Has the age of the polymath passed? Is education too specialised to accommodate the person who is filled with curiosity about the world and who wants to know a lot about a lot?

From the Journal

A new road sign has appeared: 'Dead Slow – Pedestrians in the Road due to Social Distancing.'

I visited Minchinhampton this morning to pick up medication from the chemist. The town was busy with people queuing outside shops, everyone keeping the regulation distance apart, even darting into the road to avoid passing each other too closely. I collected my order very quickly from Boots, there was no queue there, posted some letters and then was hit by an overwhelming longing for normality. What a joy it would be to meet friends for a coffee and chat without the need for masks or distancing.

> a woman with child
> smiles from two metres away
> swifts wheel overhead

Minchinhampton Common has been a godsend. A wide open space where we can walk as far as we want without worrying about pinch points where the two metre rule could be easily transgressed. Today the breeze fills the air with the sounds of horse riders chatting accompanied by the creaking of leather saddles and tack, the swish of horse tails and the muffled sound of hooves on grass.

Years ago, I was walking our dog on the common very early one morning when a horse and rider appeared out of the mist. The horse was pale grey and the rider was dressed in flowing clothes from a more romantic era. Like Rhiannon outrunning Pwyll she passed 'swiftly but without haste'. Time slipped and I was transported to a dream world where such things are possible.

Early morning mists give the common a mystery it loses once the air clears but it has enough of its own mythical potential with its prehistoric field systems and defensive bulwarks to seed the imagination.

We spot more people. An elderly couple followed by parents with children, they all wave cheerfully.

> each walker we pass
> smiles – the distance between us
> still keeps us legal

For part of our route we walk a stretch of ancient pathway that appears and disappears at random; its original destination is no longer evident and fewer people walk here these days. Only the scuff of our boots on the stones disturbs the silence until we are back on grass again. The shade of the trees holds us for a moment to cool down and drink some water before we are out in the sun once more.

> the broken paving
> frees grass to grow here and there
> this path to nowhere

Oriental Plane
(*Platanus orientalis*)

If you have visited Greece you probably sat under an Oriental plane tree. Their branches provide cool shade on the hottest of days. Plato and Horace recommended it as a place to sit and drink while keeping out of the sun. More diligent people also appreciated it: there is a legend that Hippocrates taught his students under a plane tree on the island of Kos. In fact, there is reported to be a piece of that very tree still growing in one of the squares of Kos town.

An Oriental plane planted in the grounds of Corsham Court by Lancelot 'Capability' Brown in 1760 has been identified as having the largest single spread of any tree in the UK. At 64 metres it is thought to spread over an area consistent with a football pitch. Since 2008, Bath Spa University has had facilities in Corsham Court and I wonder if any of the students who sit in the shade of that Oriental plane feel a connection with those early Greek medical students.

It is one of the parents of the London plane, the other being the American sycamore, also known as occidental plane, buttonwood or water beech. Arborists like to keep us on our toes!

>sipping Metaxa
>talking of past holidays
>under a plane tree

Paperbark Maple
(*Acer griseum*)

>orange cinnamon
>bark like the Martian landscape
>beautiful naked

Looking for ideas to create interesting walks in winter I thought of the paperbark maple. Curls of the paper-thin bark peel off the trunk and branches and could be missed when the tree is in full leaf but in winter, when its leaves have fallen to the ground, the bark is revealed in all its glory.

The seeds are winged, like so many maple seeds. Nicknamed helicopters by children or sometimes called keys, they are one of the marvels of the tree world. The wings catch the breeze and are whirled away from the parent tree to grow elsewhere and successfully colonise a favourable area.

>carried far away
>the seed begins a new life
>beyond the parent

The plant hunter Ernest Wilson brought this species to the UK from China in 1901, along with over a thousand other plants. So many plants that bring pleasure to the British gardener came from far away and were once the reason these plant hunters travelled and sometimes put their lives at risk.

Indian Cedar
(*Cedrus deodara*)

These are classed as a signature species in the National Arboretum at Westonbirt. They contribute to the character of the arboretum and are planted to create a unique landscape.

> Indian cedar
> thought curative and sacred
> sieves the morning sun

Deodar is Sanskrit for 'wood of the gods' and it is native to parts of Afghanistan, Pakistan and India as well as other regions around the Himalaya. The houseboats of Kashmir were made of this rot-resistant wood and it has been used to build temples, bridges and the more prosaic public buildings. It is aromatic, anti-fungal and insect repellent and is ideal for storage. It is also used in Ayurvedic medicine to treat conditions such as eczema and psoriasis, diarrhoea and dysentery.

There is a large sacred grove of *C. deodara* near the Indian hill town of Shimla. People who walk through the grove will dust off their clothes before leaving it to ensure they take nothing that belongs to the deity. This sort of reverence must be partially responsible for the prevention of destruction and the healthy number of the trees in that area.

> the wood of the gods
> touch but take nothing with you
> just serenity

From the Journal

Time hangs heavy but we are adjusting and now take more interest in the changes. Many people will not venture out of their houses to shop and have to depend on neighbours, friends and family to shop for essentials and to deliver them. There are also professional couriers who will bring food and other goods.

>the man in blue gloves
>drives his van through the village
>watched by a lone cat
>
>he leaves groceries,
>knocks and walks away
>kindness personified

We are also more aware of strangers in our road; they turn out to be family members who are checking up on their older relatives. There is a feeling of communities melding at a distance. We call out – how are you? Do you need anything? We smile and walk on when reassured that all is well.

>Nothing much to do
>'stay home, stay safe,' our mantra
>Thursdays we let loose.
>
>the sound of applause
>mingling with spoons hitting pans –
>caring with neighbours

On Thursdays we emerge like moles to wave and applaud in appreciation of all those on the front line. The nurses, doctors, cleaners, porters and many others who we realise are daily risking their lives to care for the ill and sit with the dying.

On the news we hear of an elderly man who is walking in his garden to raise money for the NHS, something noble and touching to watch.

>we cheer for you too,
>old hero, walking, walking.
>friends will meet again

Unable to meet in person and with a friend now marooned in Spain as travel is banned, we discover Zoom and have Sunday coffee mornings to share drinks and cakes ethereally.

>smiling and waving
>disembodied, separate
>virtual friendship

Maidenhair Tree
(*Ginkgo biloba*)

The only surviving member of its genus, the ginkgo would have felt dinosaurs brushing past it in the Jurassic period and watched their extinction as the world changed.

It is amongst a number of trees given the title of Hibakujumoku by the Japanese to denote they survived the dropping of the atomic bomb on Hiroshima. The bits of the plants above ground were destroyed but the roots survived to produce new trees. A wonderful project, Green Legacy Hiroshima, sends seeds from these 'survivor' trees all over the world to be grown as a sign of peace and regeneration.

There are many claims made for the medicinal efficacy of the ginkgo: that it improves circulation, aids memory, supports vision and eye health, improves asthma and a host of other conditions. Whether any of these claims are true is the subject of medical research.

The leaves exhibit dichotomous venation – each vein radiates out from the base of the leaf, never forming a network. This is unique and, to my mind, creates a very elegant form.

Another interesting word for you – *dioecious* – meaning they have separate male and female trees. Most of the ginkgo trees you see in parks and gardens are males; the seeds of the female tree are described as very attractive but smelling like vomit! I suppose somewhere in the country someone must be braving this smell otherwise where would little ginkgo trees come from?

    perfectly formed leaf
    even when it is seen close up
    Ginkgo biloba

Western Red Cedar
(*Thuja plicata*)

Not a true cedar at all but a member of the cypress family and, like so many trees, it has aliases: giant red cedar, Pacific red cedar, shinglewood, canoe cedar to name but a few. I very much like the Native American name for it which translates as 'long life maker'.

Wood from the Western red cedar can be seen in part of the Senedd in Cardiff and First Nations people on the Pacific Coast of North America have used it for housing, totem poles, canoes and a host of other items for generations. Some of the coastal tribes refer to themselves as 'people of the red cedar'. Before it is felled for use by the local tribes a small ceremony is performed to show respect.

One of the legends that surround this tree comes from the culture of the Coast Salish people; it says that there was once a very generous man who gave the people whatever they needed and when he died the Great Spirit declared that a red cedar tree would grow from his burial site and be useful to all people, providing clothing and shelter. And so it does.

On one of our walks we came across a Muslim family quietly laying out prayer mats; a tranquil and sacred moment.

> off the narrow path
> voices surround the cedar
> a family prays

Box Elder
(*Acer negundo*)

Living seventy-five to a hundred years, this is a relatively short-lived tree with brittle wood and a tendency to drop branches. Some people use its high sugar content sap to produce a syrup not unlike maple syrup. The leaves are sometimes confused with poison ivy but it is not related and does not have the same nasty effect when touched. Some people have been known to plant it around their property in the hopes that others will think it is poison ivy and stay well away!

Its drooping racemes appear in spring and are beautiful when viewed in full sunlight and, when its time has come, the wood can be used for turning bowls and other decorative articles.

It is a native of North America where it is classed as a riparian species most often found along watercourses. It is neither an elder nor a box but the common name indicates its leaves resemble elder (*Sambucus*) and its pale wood is similar to that of the box (*Buxus sempervirens*).

> avoided and feared
> mistaken identity
> can serve a purpose

From the Journal

News today that David's godfather Clem has died. Although he was ninety-seven it still comes as a bit of a shock. He lived a long and very active life until the past few years. We remember him fondly and laugh at some of his observations on life, politics, television, sport and even crop circles – don't ask!

The nursing home where Clem spent his last few weeks is filled with heroic staff. It is heartening to know there are such people in the world. They have kept this virus at bay and we are comforted to know that Clem died from the frailty of old age rather than Covid-19.

There is now the challenge of organising a funeral during Lockdown. There are various restrictions imposed by the government, which includes travelling any distance, that makes such things as registering a death and organising the funeral rather more difficult than usual.

Wednesday 20th May 2020

The lane to the crematorium is long and winding. We have an idea of where the place is but still manage to miss the entrance and have to turn round in Shepton Mallet and approach it from the other direction. The rules put in place by the government mean that we are not able to invite Clem's wide circle of friends to join us in the funeral and we are not allowed to sit with others not of our household. There are only eight of us present.

> distanced in households
> he would have loved a full house
> we few paid tribute

[I must add – in January 2022, it has come to light that on that very day the prime minister and his colleagues had a lovely bring-your-own-bottle garden party for 30–40 people. This news leaves a very bitter taste in the mouth and we can only hope there is some accounting for this flouting of the rules that we were all told to obey by those very people.]

Funeral over we head to Wells for Dave to visit Clem's solicitor. There are plenty of spaces in the car park and we find one shaded by a tree. A house faces on to the car park and I am amused to see it is called Bay View. I can see neither the sea nor a bay tree nearby.

>from a sycamore
>a single chaffinch singing
>to a mobile phone

Wednesday 15th July 2020

On our drive down to the church at Henton, where Clem's ashes are to be interred, we both commented on how this would be the last time we come this way to see Clem. After so many years it will feel quite strange not to visit him in his little bungalow overlooking fields and the Mendip Hills beyond.

There were three of us who knew Clem well: Clem's long-time friend and home help Jayne, David, and me standing at the graveside. The vicar was young and had created a lovely 'service' for the occasion. Clem's ashes were placed alongside those of his late wife, Betty, in the little churchyard not far from their home. I placed a few dark pink roses as a small tribute to mark the spot. The headstone will be updated with his name and dates when the mason can do the job. We had a feeling of closure as we left but we will certainly miss him.

brushing leaves away
this new bunch of pink roses
brightens a sad day

Over the two years that this book covers, and since Clem died, several more friends and family members passed away. Like so many others we have not been able to attend those funerals in person where numbers are restricted but have managed to view proceedings via the Internet. What a strange experience.

Bhutan Pine
(*Pinus wallichiana*)

Alias the blue pine, Himalayan pine and a lot of now invalid botanical names; we keep noticing that names of trees can be tricky to get right.

It is native to an area stretching from Afghanistan to China but now can be found in landscapes all over the world.

The Bhutan pine is farmed for its resin that can be distilled to produce turpentine. Long thin needles that grow in bundles of five are a lovely blue grey colour, which makes it a popular tree for planting in parks and larger gardens.

> a morning well spent
> walking through trees in the rain
> the scent of Bhutan

The *wallichiana* part of the name comes from the Danish botanist and surgeon, Nathanial Wallich, who brought the seeds to Britain in the nineteenth century. He has lots of plants named after him and even a pheasant... the cheer pheasant, which is described as 'lacking in colour but making up for that in noise when it gets excited.' A bit like some of us!

Juniper
(*Juniperus communis*)

This tree can claim to form the highest known treeline on earth – at around 16,000 feet in the Himalaya.

If you like gin you will easily recognise the smell of juniper. The word 'gin' comes from jenever the Dutch word for juniper . . . or genevrier in French.

Some of you might be familiar with the Grimm story of the Juniper Tree. If you have not yet read it be prepared for murder, cannibalism and child abuse. It has a strangely 'happy ever after' ending in a way only the Brothers Grimm could come up with.

Burning juniper wood has been part of rituals for generations, to purify buildings and drive away demons, to fuel the Beltane fires between which livestock is driven to purify them and to create incense that is used to manifest things from beyond this world.

The juniper came to Britain around 10,000 years ago as the glaciers of the Ice Age melted and is thus regarded as one of our three native conifers, the other two being yew and Scots pine. We had a juniper in our front garden, bought as a 'dwarf' juniper it remained a manageable size for about ten years, then it grew like mad and covered almost the whole of the lawn. It was impressive but not what we thought we had bought. Eventually it succumbed to some sort of disease, perhaps a form of phytophthora, and died very quickly.

The gin and tonic we are familiar with was a way of colonial Brits taking the tonic water that contained quinine and which helped prevent malaria – at least that was their excuse.

Gin is a favourite ingredient in many a cocktail – below are just three ideas, it's up to you to measure and create. Cheers!

gin, orange liqueur
lemon, sugar, choice of fizz
French 75

gin and sweet vermouth
Campari and orange zest
makes a Negroni

mint leaves and lime juice
shake well with gin and syrup
Mojito – gin style

From the Journal

Being at home so much has made me more aware of life inside and out. We catch glimpses of neighbours, talk to them at a distance and have learnt to appreciate when some things continue as 'normal'. Children playing in the road compensate for the lack of movement in the mornings as people no longer head out to work.

your breath in the night
brings me awake once again
and I am happy

a silent morning
no one leaves for work today
no child leaves for school

'A strange spring,' she said.
'Primroses, bluebells, crocus
do not bring me joy.'

another month gone –
wine in a glass in my hand
nothing on my feet

What's that noise outside?
Shouting, laughing, loud music.
Oh . . . their energy!

wobbling on his bike
the small boy squeals with delight
now he shows no fear

a gin and tonic
memories of holidays
a pip spoils the dream

a morning baking
scent: maple syrup, orange.
My oven's humming

broken reverie
what might have been decided
without the phone call?

Zoom coffee mornings
wearing smart clothes for one hour
to look nice for you

green tea or normal?
leaves or bags in the teapot?
as it comes, he says.

time for tea, he says.
meaning sandwiches and cakes
not just a hot drink.

I searched everywhere
to locate that faint fragrance.
not flowers – hand-wash!

dozy afternoon
a day dream includes your voice
years after you died

VE Day 8th May 2020

We are given permission to hold street parties as long as we adhere to the rules. Social distancing means we stand or sit in family groups with the odd foray into someone else's space but still keeping 2 metres apart.

Remembering people who lived through wars gives me food for thought. Their resilience is inspiring and I remember my parents talking about their experiences of watching bombs fall on Swansea, living with rationing and the frantic need to live life to the full while they could.

stay-home-street-party
spent the day making bunting
remembering Dad

Silent lane

VE Day

Enkianthus campanulatus

Prickly Myrtle

Wire Netting Bush
(*Corokia cotoneaster*)

A strange looking shrub, it has the appearance of someone who just can't make their mind up which way to go. Its stems wriggle about all over the place, sometimes intertwining sometimes changing direction to create a zig-zag pattern. It comes from New Zealand, so maybe it finds living up here in the Northern Hemisphere confusing. *Corokia* is derived from the Maori name, *Korokio*.

> truly transplanted
> do they sing your long journey
> across the oceans

Its appearance is obviously the origin of the English name for this sculptural shrub. As well as using it for hedging, some people used the wooden twigs and branches to create hooks for fishing or to create an instrument that could pierce skin for reasons good or ill. In spring it is covered with small vibrant yellow flowers.

> growing left then right
> so many choices to make
> that *Corokia*

Incense Cedar
(*Calocedrus decurrans*)

Not a true cedar – that would be too easy – but another member of the cypress family. Its wood is used to make a certain writing implement with which we are all familiar from childhood. Next time you are in the Lake District pop into the Derwent Pencil Museum. Keswick, so the legend goes, is the home of the first pencil. They boast miniature pencil sculptures, an 8-metre colouring pencil and the Queen's Diamond Jubilee pencil.

The most interesting and thought provoking exhibits are the special pencils made during the Second World War. In 1942 Charles Fraser Smith of MI9 (thought to be the inspiration for Q in Fleming's James Bond books) came to the factory with a request. He wanted pencils that could contain secret maps and compasses to give out to Lancaster Bomber airmen to help them evade capture when they were shot down. The maps indicated a variety of escape routes out of occupied territory.

under the cedars
a child sharpens her pencil
memories of school

It is another of the Westonbirt Arboretum signature species and has a role in creating the unique character of the arboretum. They are often planted in groups but there are also single trees dotted around the site and, while they do not smell of incense, they can have the evocative smell that you get when you sharpen a pencil.

Seven Son Flower
(*Heptacodium miconioides*)

Bit of a misnomer, since there are actually only six flowers in a ring, the seventh bud-like structure in the middle is the rachis which sometimes pushes through the flower and creates another ring of flowers above the original. The flowers are small and white and fragrant, just as you would expect a member of the honeysuckle family to be. Once the flowers fade and fall there is another show of rosy-red calyces that last into autumn and brighten up a dull day.

It is from China and is classed as 'vulnerable' by the International Union for Conservation of Nature. Vulnerable describes plants or animals that are likely to become endangered if nothing is done to improve the circumstances that are presently threatening their survival in the wild. More often than not this is habitat destruction.

>flowers in a ring
>catching the last of the rain
>did you notice them

Serbian Spruce
(*Picea omorika*)

This graceful tree is classified as endangered by the IUCN in its native Drina River valley in the limestone mountains of western Serbia and eastern Bosnia and Herzegovina. In February 2020 a conference was held in the area to look at ways of ensuring that the tree does not disappear from its homeland. This will be done by improving the management of the threatened habitat and raising awareness. It is sobering to think about how much work is needed all over the world to repair the damage that has been done to so many tree species and habitats.

Perhaps it is also a sign of hope when people who were warring as recently as 1992 and suffering terrible atrocities during a campaign of ethnic cleansing might be brought together in the effort to save the Picea omorika.

> unhealed wounds are deep
> the road to recovery
> lies under the trees

Tall and slender, they are often used in landscaped parks and gardens to create a contrast to trees that spread. Its cones turn from purple to red/brown as the tree matures and hang from the tips of the branches that cascade down the main trunk. It looks like an elegant Christmas tree, but as it grows to a height of 50 or 60 feet, the dilemma you might face is how to get the star onto the top.

Dawn Redwood
(*Metasequoia glyptostroboides*)

Described variously as a living fossil or dinosaur tree, this is another species that was thought only to exist as fossils until the 1940s when living specimens were found in China. Unlike other redwoods it is deciduous and loses its needles in the autumn. During my research into trees I come across words that are new to me and the new word found when reading about the dawn redwood is geomancy which seems to be related to feng shui. It is thought that a tree was protected in one community in China because of its auspicious position in the environment.

> winter dawn redwood
> carpets the ground with colour
> standing where it should

In the past, plant hunters went out to distant parts of the world, gathered seeds and specimens and brought them back to great acclaim, passing through borders with no problems. In these more enlightened times there is more care taken, particularly by some countries with unique flora and fauna, to stop alien species being introduced into their environment. This is good in many respects but can give researchers several obstacles to cope with.

An interesting story is recorded in *Arnoldia*, the magazine of the Arnold Arboretum of Harvard University. In 1948 Ralph Chaney, professor of palaeontology at the University of California, Berkeley, brought back seeds and four seedlings from a trip to China. He hid the seeds when going through customs on arrival in Hawaii but an inspector from the Plant and Economic Quarantine in Honolulu demanded that the seedlings be destroyed. Chaney argued, becoming almost hysterical, shouting that the trees were priceless and more than a million years old . . . 'millions of years, tens of millions of years, a hundred million years'. Eventually the inspector agreed that, since they were more than a hundred and fifty years old they could officially be declared antiques and allowed through!

It is still classified as endangered but that's better than extinct.

From the Journal

These days of restricted socialising has had the effect of allowing many more memories than usual to come to mind. On occasion, when the mornings have been bright and fresh, we have both mentioned the times when we lived in Tunis and the memories come flooding back. What a great place to begin married life. We lived in a tiny villa surrounded by a small garden filled with orange trees, geraniums, hibiscus, honeysuckle and jasmine. We had a peach tree and watched its one fruit avidly as it grew and ripened, anticipating the day when we could eat a peach grown in our own garden. One morning we woke and went out to inspect our crop only to find it lying on the ground half nibbled away by an early bird. We still feel that disappointment all these years later.

> here they come again
> surfing on my memories
> those clamouring ghosts

Today I was looking at a photo of one of the smaller canals in Venice and felt a great longing to be sitting at an outdoor café and having grilled fish delivered to my table by a cheerful waiter. It would not have to be Venice just a place where the locals speak passionate Italian, wave their arms around and dress to impress. I wonder when, if ever, that will happen again. We have recently been counting our blessings; travelling to beautiful places, living in interesting countries without, perhaps, realising just how lucky we were.

the muezzin calling
honeysuckle and jasmine
conjure up our past

we laughed and we danced
fed each other ripe peaches
remember that, love?

Monkey Puzzle
(*Araucaria araucana*)

I had always believed that Whitby jet was formed by the decomposition and compression of wood from the family Araucaria and could have told you a lot about how Queen Victoria wore it when mourning Prince Albert, etc., etc. But now I find that some early research might disprove that theory as it suggests that jet is not formed from the Araucaria family after all! I await more information.

In the meantime let's get back to the monkey puzzle, sometimes called the chilean pine. Almost reptilian in appearance, it is another tree that is easy to imagine being the backdrop for *Jurassic Park*. Its tough leaves look a little like scales and are sharp to the touch. It shares a common ancestry with the wollemi pine of Australia from a time when Australia, Antarctica and South America were part of the super continent of Gondwana. To learn about trees you have to get used to a very different time scale.

It produces large cones full of seeds which provide food for rodents, birds and people, all of which help to spread the seeds far and wide.

> they're too sharp to climb
> the children scamper away
> monkey puzzle trees

Common Beech
(*Fagus sylvatica*)

You have probably seen beech trees or hedges with their brown leaves on throughout winter as if they are reluctant to let them go. Holding on to leaves like that is called marcescence and occurs in lots of other trees – oak, hornbeam and some willows. This habit is useful in beech hedges as they remain a good screen even in winter.

> sharply pointed buds
> copper brown hiding new growth
> the beech waits for spring

The copper or purple beech is a mutation and was first recorded in the seventeenth century in Germany. It is thought that 99 per cent of copper beeches today are descendants of this German ancestor.

Some people use the young leaves of the beech to make something called beech leaf noyau and beech leaf gin infusion. Recipes are available on the internet. I haven't tried them myself but have read positive reports from those who have.

The soft bark of the beech can be easily carved and archaeologists find arborglyphs made by naval surveyors marking out trees to be used for shipbuilding, concentric circles known as 'witches' marks' to ward off evil spirits and the initials of lovers. The New Forest National Park Authority is recording the marks, some of which date back to the sixteenth century, before they fade and change as the tree grows.

There is a legend that Ogma, the Irish goddess who is supposed to have invented the ogham alphabet, first carved it on a beech tree.

The cellulose extracted from beech pulp is used to create a textile called modal, a semisynthetic material that is biodegradable. As the search for materials to replace those made with fossil fuels goes on, we will no doubt learn that trees can step in to save us from ourselves – as long as we don't destroy our biosphere before we understand what resources we have.

Holly
(*Ilex aquifolium*)

that ancient carol –
'the holly bears a berry
red as any blood'
Christians and Pagans sing
of rebirth and joy

The holly has to be one of our most familiar trees, even if you have not seen a real one you will have seen plenty around Christmas time – plastic wreaths and garlands, on Christmas cards or on wrapping paper. With its bright red berries and dark shiny, spiky leaves, it is very striking. In winter the tree is often plundered by people who want to use it to 'deck the halls with boughs of holly' as instructed by the carol.

It can live for around 300 years and remains green all year round. Male and female trees carry small white flowers during the springtime and, once pollinated by insects, the female flowers develop into red berries that can remain throughout winter.

The mistle thrush is a great fan of these berries and will guard them from other birds but the berries also provide vital food for wood mice and dormice in winter – if they can get a look in. The leaves are eaten by caterpillars of the holly blue butterfly as well as other butterflies and moths. The interdependence of species is a lesson to us all.

Over the years, the holly tree has been regarded as a charm against the devil and as a symbol of fertility and it was considered unlucky to cut one down. However, if it does succumb to the axe, holly provides the palest of all woods and was often used to make furniture and walking sticks.

European Larch
(*Larix decidua*)

Becoming broader with age, the larch shares some characteristics with humans, even developing fissures in its pinkish-brown bark as the years pass.

It looks like an evergreen but sheds its needles in winter; they turn a glorious yellow before they fall and the ground beneath the trees becomes a stunning golden carpet. Because they lose their foliage, the sunlight can penetrate the trees which enables spring flowers to flourish beneath them.

Pollinated by the wind, the female cones grow brown then open their scales to release winged seeds to fly away. Seeds are eaten by red squirrels, siskins, and redpolls while black grouse help themselves to the buds. Moth caterpillars feed on the leaves and the larch tortrix moth caterpillars will eat the scales of the cones.

Like so many other trees, the larch is said to protect us against evil spirits or becoming victims of a spell.

>bringing us fresh hope
>new life appears with each spring
>beneath the larches

From the Journal

In our downstairs cloakroom we have a poster from the 1970 Bath Festival of Blues and Progressive Music. Just reading the names: Steppenwolf, Pink Floyd, Led Zeppelin, Moody Blues, Fairport Convention, Johnny Winter, can transport us to student days when we hitch-hiked from Swansea to fields near Shepton Mallet to join thousands of others for a weekend of music.

> a much younger me
> on the threshold of a dream –
> oh, those Moody Blues

We'd agreed to meet friends and share their tent – you can't miss us, the tent is green and very new – ha!! On arrival we realised almost every tent was new and green so we just found a spot on the ground, chosen for its distance from the stage and sound system, and declared it ours for the duration.

The sun shone, then it rained and then the sun came out again. The music was brilliant, people around us were friendly and we managed not to lose each other whenever one of us needed the loo! I seem to remember someone had put a cabbage on a pole not far from our spot so we used that to navigate whenever we had to move around the crowd. Thank God it was a manky looking cabbage and not something edible.

I remember Hell's Angels down by the stage. Never having seen so many of them in one place before, it was scary and exciting at the same time. Rumours went round of them beating people up, selling drugs and a host of other unsavoury activities. They took over the area in front of the stage and became 'security' for the event. Most of us gave them a wide berth, even some of the real security guys avoided upsetting them.

There were announcements about adulterated drugs doing the rounds and warnings not to take them – acid if my memory serves! John Peel and Mike Raven's voices sounded thin and melancholic in between the shrieking guitar riffs, drum rolls and vocals of the groups coming through banks of speakers that looked like black cliffs on either side of the stage.

Night and day, day and night, half sleeping, half waking, each group morphing into the next and Donovan taking the stage when someone could not arrive on time. Is this really a memory or a dream of a memory or maybe just the threshold of a dream?

> that rock festival
> memories of youth 'well' spent
> keep us going now

Western Hemlock
(*Tsuga heterophylla*)

The needles of the Western hemlock are surprisingly soft but so dense that the tree casts a heavy shade which means the ground beneath it has little chance of supporting much flora. The needles have white stripes on the underside and, when crushed, give off a scent which is similar to the unrelated poisonous hemlock plant. The trees grow to over 50 metres tall and the tips of their branches droop gracefully to avoid the build-up of snow which could break them.

It forms something called an ectomycorrhizal association with a variety of fungi and there is a lot of research into these symbiotic relationships to learn where they fit into ecosystems and how our activity might be affecting the status quo. There has been concern over trees in Washington State dying off due to drought causing an opportunist fungal pathogen to move in and kill off the trees. Since the Western Hemlock is their state tree people are very concerned and hope that wetter conditions will redress the balance.

I have read that preparations from the bark of this tree have been used to treat lice, T.B. and even syphilis in the past. It has been difficult to find out just how effective this treatment was.

>we see the trees die
>so much we do not know
>when rain goes missing

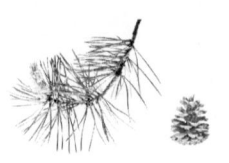

Scots Pine
(*Pinus sylvestris*)

This is our only native pine and one of our three native conifers. It thrives on poor soil and forms swathes of the Caledonian pine forest in Scotland. In that forest it shares its environment with two wonderfully named rare orchids: creeping lady's tresses and the lesser twayblade. It is not confined to Scotland though and can be found growing naturally in Siberia, Scandinavia and Spain making it the most widely distributed conifer in the world.

In 2014 it was voted Scotland's national tree.

In the UK farmers have used it as a windbreak around their fields and, in the past, it was planted along the old drovers' roads as a way of marking the routes. More romantically, it has been planted where warriors and chieftains were buried. Apparently, even further back in history, druids lit fires of Scots pine at the winter solstice to encourage the sun to return.

I have found it difficult to recognise firs, pines and cypresses without consulting a book or app to confirm my thoughts but the one thing that helps with the Scots pine is the way the younger bark differs from the old. When the tree is mature the lower bark is brown, but look up to the new growth and you will spot it glowing amber particularly when the sun shines.

Over the years the resin has been used to make turpentine and, along with an infusion of the needles, as an inhalant to relieve respiratory problems. Its tall, straight trunk has been used for ships' masts and the timber used for furniture, pit props and fence posts. Even the cones are useful – they can be used to produce dye or, when dried, as kindling to start a fire.

beneath the Scots pines
so the old stories tell us
sleeping warriors

Shagbark Hickory
(*Carya ovata*)

As the name implies, this tree, when mature, has a noticeably shaggy bark. Hickory itself is a corruption of the Virginia Algonquian word *pawcohiccora*, which was a type of milk made by indigenous people from hickory nuts. The early European immigrants observed the indigenous people pounding the nuts to make this liquid and also using the oils from the nuts for cooking and medicine.

It is a member of the walnut family and the sweet nuts it produces are eaten by squirrels and people but, because the trees take a long time to produce the nuts and cannot be relied upon to produce good crops year on year, they are not often grown for commercial purposes.

There are recipes online for 'shagbark hickory syrup' which can be used as a substitute for maple syrup and does not entail tapping the tree. One recipe I found suggested mixing it with equal parts of sumac infused rum as a treat!

Hickory wood has been used to make bows by the Native Americans as well as tools like axe handles, ploughs and even skis. We probably know it more as a wood that is used for smoking meat.

> a New World indeed
> not knowing how to survive
> they had much to learn

Prickly Myrtle
(*Rhaphitham spinosus*)

Despite having a name that would not look out of place for a villain in a 1960s-era comic, this member of the verbena family is very attractive especially when covered in purple-blue fruits. It is certainly prickly – the spines are long and very sharp which might explain why the berries seem untouched by birds.

Walking through trees on a summer's day it is a real delight to find this tree. The berries glow against the dark evergreen foliage and you know that they will be there until the middle of winter. In spring the tree provides colour with its violet flowers that look like little trumpets.

> even in winter
> amongst dark leaves and sharp spines
> myrtle berries glow

It originates from South America where its fruits are believed to be an antidote to some extremely dangerous hallucinogenic plants that are used by shaman to enter trance states.

From the Journal

The sky, without the usual contrails left by aircraft, is a vivid blue and it can be easy to forget why it is so blue. Our planned trip to Cape Cod to Daniel and Tracey's wedding has been cancelled. There must be millions of us changing our plans, missing so much and so much.

> silence in the skies
> how many thought to travel
> stay home stay safe – stay

Some neighbours have put their 'holiday' energies into gardening, now that their outdoor space has become even more precious.

> your garden's perfect
> hedges trimmed lawn mowed no weeds
> mine runs wild and free

To the NHS & others

> three more weeks Lockdown.
> how we all thirst for freedom
> while you thirst for rest.

> you held a cold hand
> and now you hold your own child
> yawning in the sun

> it takes time to dress
> to shut out chance encounters
> to keep your child safe

Is there a point to all of the news every day? It is heralded by grim numbers of those who have died and each number is someone who had dreams, hopes, families and a place in the world. Whilst I have some sympathy for those politicians who are faced with the challenges of this pandemic, I can't help but see the way so many of them have been promoted beyond their abilities. There are others who might be able but who cannot move away from their habit of protecting themselves come what may. Why do they find it so hard to say sorry or I don't know? Why do they cast around to find someone to blame rather than finding ways of learning from mistakes and misunderstandings?

> under the spotlight
> the politician stutters
> knowing he is wrong

Sweet Chestnut
(*Castanea sativa*)

One of the strongest autumn and winter memories from my childhood is of men roasting chestnuts over a glowing brazier. Every market would have at least one and it was a joy to buy a little paper bag full of blackened chestnuts and try to peel them without burning your fingers.

The tree is often cultivated to produce nuts that can be used for roasting, grinding into flour or creating desserts. Chestnut stuffing often makes an appearance at Christmas to accompany the turkey or goose.

It is thought that the sweet chestnut was introduced to Britain by the Romans as it is native to the east Mediterranean where the Greeks dedicated it to the god Zeus. The oldest known tree is to be found on Mount Etna, Sicily, and is thought to be between 2,000 and 4,000 years old.

The fungus, *Cryphonectria parasitica* or sweet chestnut blight, has arrived in Britain and is thought to have spread through imported infected plants. This and other instances of disease illustrate a clear need for some sort of biosecurity where imported plants are concerned. We live in global times as the current human pandemic proves so it will probably prove impossible to prevent every transfer of pathogen in plants and animals.

The wood is used for furniture making and its resistance to rot makes it ideal for fence posts.

> the child will forget
> cold winds and frozen fingers
> when roasting chestnuts

Angelica
(*Aralia spinose*)

Is it a tree or a shrub or a 'trub'? The plant can't decide what it is. I leave that conundrum to the reader to solve.

Sometimes it is known as the devil's walking stick because of the extremely sharp spines it carries on its stems and leaf mid-ribs. Its compound leaves can be up to a metre long and half a metre wide making them some of the largest leaves of a temperate tree species.

Bees and butterflies are the main pollinators, coming in large numbers to the tiny flowers and, in turn, the berries attract flocks of birds.

It belongs to the ginseng family but is not reported to have quite the same energy-boosting properties as other members. It has been used by indigenous peoples of North America as an anti-inflammatory to treat aching joints. One way of doing that is to infuse the berries in brandy but, as with all the suggested uses in this book, I cannot guarantee the safety or efficacy of these remedies and would always suggest further research.

I believe the angelica that is used in baking is from the *Angelica archangelica* rather than the devil's walking stick variety.

> some thought the devil
> in need of a walking stick
> you fitted the bill

Atlas Cedar
(*Cedrus atlantica*)

From the Atlas Mountains in Morocco and Algeria this is a beautiful tree. When I see it I try to conjure up the image of forests sweeping down the mountains and creating a swathe of green against the ochre earth.

As with so many forests there has been a lot of damage caused by human activity over the years but Morocco has a reforestation programme to redress the balance, which is heartening. We are all learning to respect trees and their place in our world, and whilst we can't control wild fires we can try to mitigate their effects and the devastation we cause by harvesting timber in such huge amounts.

I read that the previous US president, Jimmy Carter, had a treehouse built for his daughter in an Atlas cedar growing in the grounds of the White House and he had it built in such a way that it did not interfere with the growth of the tree, showing a respect we do not always associate with the modern world.

The fragrant wood of the Atlas cedar is sometimes used to build wardrobes and drawers for storing clothes.

There is a lovely variation of the Atlas cedar, the blue Atlas cedar – *Cedrus atlantica glauca*, which is the more common sight in parks and gardens because of its attractive colour.

> take blue from the sky
> mix with dark Moroccan green
> to transform the park
> with blue Atlas cedar trees –
> now reforest its homeland

Roble Beech
(*Nothofagus obliqua/Lophozonia obliqua*)

Some of these trees are like villains with a host of aliases. The roble beech is a false beech, also known as the roble pellin, Patagonian oak (*roble* means 'oak' in Spanish) and, of course, it is not a true oak either!

According to Henry John Elwes and Augustine Henry's book, *The Trees of Great Britain and Ireland*, this tree was introduced to this country in 1849 but died out and was reintroduced by Elwes in 1902. Perhaps its dislike of very cold weather caused the first demise of the species in the UK as it now seems to have taken hold in some of the milder areas of the country.

These days we worry about importing plants without taking great care to ensure they will not bring pests and diseases that will attack our native flora but in the days of the plant hunters this was not an issue. Many of the trees and plants we now think of as typical of the British countryside have come to us from all over the world.

>   a moment of calm
>   to remember those now lost
>   as rain drops from leaves

From the Journal

One aspect of watching the news is that we learn new words or phrases, some accessible and others completely mindboggling. Amongst the obvious – social bubble, superforecaster, covidiot and doomscrolling, I found a new favourite word, *quarantini*, which is an alcoholic drink sipped at home during Lockdown. I haven't found a recipe so I guess you please yourself with your chosen tipple.

> to navigate now
> we need a new language
> neologisms

Technology, if you have it, has made this whole experience easier. Families can meet up in a virtual world, some can continue to work and others find new hobbies or take up forms of exercise in the privacy of their own living rooms. There is so much positivity in its role but, emojis! I have used them myself, the thumbs-up 'like' symbol, the laugh out loud symbol and so on, but please, please stop with the crying one. Far better to write a word or two than to send this to someone who is in need of sympathy and/or empathy.

> crying emoji –
> no substitute for real words
> to say 'I am here'

Bishop Pine
(*Pinus muricata*)

Occurring naturally in coastal California but has transplanted successfully in Britain. There is a theory that it was given its common name because it was first discovered growing near the Catholic mission of San Luis Obispo de Tolosa in 1832.

Its cones have tiny, sharp spines on them and that gives it another common name, the prickle cone pine! These spines mean that the squirrels that would like to feed on the seeds have a difficult time getting at them. The cones might stay closed for years, opening after a fire or on very hot days; trees that need high temperatures to shed their seeds like that are called 'pyrophites'. This type of reproduction results in stands of trees that are all the same age because the seeds were released at the same time during the same fire.

The wood is strong, coarse grained and is often used in pulping and papermaking.

On the coast, its roots are very good at stabilising the soil and sand dunes, which makes it a very valuable plant in that regard. It has evolved to be able to withstand salt laden winds where other trees would fail.

> seeds within each cone
> released by a lightning strike
> to start their journey

Kyushu Lime
(*Tilia kiusiana*)

Unlike so many trees from all over the world that have been named by European plant hunters, this one was described and named in 1896 by Tomitaro Makino ('the father of Japanese botany') and his colleague Yasuyoshi Shirasawa. It is native to the south of Japan and is a very distinctive lime tree.

It is a dainty, slow growing tree with fragrant flowers that appear in August and September. Insects are attracted to these flowers and serve to pollinate the plant.

The tree was introduced into Britain in the 1930s. Sometimes described as a small shrub, it is capable of reaching heights of around 14m and more when given the right conditions and space to grow.

> *Tilia* flowers
> mark time until summer's end
> when their petals fall

Amur Maackia aka Chinese Yellow Wood
(*Maackia amurensis*)

This tree gets part of its name from the Amur River region that forms the border between northeast China and the far east of Russia. The *Maackia* epithet comes from the name of its discoverer, the nineteenth-century Russian naturalist Richard Otto Maack – sometimes known as Richard Karlovich Maack. Like so many trees, it would seem he also had an alias.

It is a member of the pea and bean family and the white pea-like flowers and dark brown pods that appear after the summer flowering attest to that membership.

Elements from this tree have been used in Asia for centuries to treat ailments including cancer. Research has discovered that the seed lectin from *Maackia amurensis* has antiviral properties and might have the potential to inhibit the serious effects of viral infections. Once again I have learned how precious our flora is in offering solutions to problems if we just take the time to investigate and preserve our ecosystem.

>with each tree we plant
>within each tree we preserve
>are secrets of life

From the Journal

Reading astronomical facts and figures, learning about new discoveries that illustrate how little we know, give me a sense of proportion. Whatever we are concerned with here on Earth does not register with the cosmos. The wonder I feel when looking at photos taken by instruments like Kepple, Hubble, the Martians we have created and other explorers we have sent out reassure me that we can, when we cooperate, achieve great things. The fact that we can still look outward while coping with this pandemic pleases me.

> cloudy brown dwarf 'star'
> six point five light years away
> with awful weather

Books, however you read them, have become even more comforting during this period. I have a Kindle which is useful at night, I can read without disturbing David by turning on a light but holding the real thing can't be beaten. So much to learn, each book brings new worlds to light and history can be brought to vivid life by a good writer.

> hidden in plain sight
> the words of our history
> in the heft of books

Just for fun I made up a three-word haiku when I read Dylan Thomas's call for us to 'Love the words'.

eventually
environmentalism
appreciated

'Love the words, the words'
Dylan Thomas calls to us
what better advice?

Service Tree
(*Sorbus domestica*)

Not to be confused with the wild service tree or the bastard service tree! The fruit of this tree has to undergo bletting, like medlars, before it is eaten. Bletting causes the fruit to lose its astringency and become pleasant to eat. Jam, juice, brandy and a type of cider are all produced from the pome. Other names for this tree are sorb tree and whitty pear.

The dense wood has been used to create wood-working planes and, more interestingly to me, wine presses.

Extracts from the tree are used by herbalists to treat a variety of conditions: vascular, lymphatic, neural and skin. As usual, there has to be a warning about consuming anything unless you know it is safe. If you want to learn more then I suggest you find a reputable source of information rather than depend on the trial and error system.

> linger after rain
> learn the meaning of patience
> time sweetens the fruit

Snowdrop Treeaka aka Silverbell Tree (*Halesia Carolina*)

The bell-shaped flowers of this deciduous tree that appear in spring are white but occasionally tinged with pink. They droop downwards and can be hidden in the foliage; the best way to see them properly is from below.

In autumn the leaves turn yellow and are followed by fruits that are pale green and have four 'wings'.

Normally growing in parts of the South Eastern United States, it is also cultivated in areas of the UK that can provide an acid or neutral soil. The Royal Horticultural Society gave it a Garden Merit Award as a successful cultivar in the UK.

Its exfoliating bark makes this the sort of tree you can find interesting all year round.

The *Halesia* part of its name is in honour of the seventeenth-century English physiologist and chemist, the Reverend Stephen Hales.

Amongst a host of other achievements the Revd Hales was the first person to measure blood pressure and invented a form of ventilator that was installed in mines and other places to improve air quality. He appears to be another polymath who found everything around him fascinating and worked to improve things where he could.

> to catch just a glimpse
> in a canopy of leaves
> stoop to find the bells

Japanese Cedar
(*Cryptomeria japonicum*)

Not a cedar at all, Japanese cedar is a member of the cypress family. It is the national tree of Japan where it is known as sugi and often planted near temples. It is an evergreen with reddish bark that can peel off and dense foliage that grows cream in the spring, then turns green in summer and bronze in autumn.

It was introduced into Britain in 1861 and is planted in large gardens where it can reach a height of 40 metres. Its branches whorl corkscrew fashion around its trunk like other cypress trees. Some varieties are pruned and wired to create bonsai versions of the tree.

Some people feel calmed after inhaling steam from water infused with its essential oil. Like many other trees, it appears to have insecticidal properties and I have seen it recommended as a deterrent for silverfish.

>confined, pruned and trained
>a forest in miniature
>the joy of bonsai

Strawberry Tree
(*Arbutus unedo*)

Named *Arbutus unedo* by Carl Linnaeus, the eighteenth-century Swedish taxonomist, in his amazing work, *Species Plantarum*. The *unedo* part of its name means 'I eat one' in Latin. There is discussion as to whether you would only want to eat one of the berries because they are not particularly tasty or so delicious you only need to eat one.

It has dark green leaves and white hermaphrodite flowers that give way to red berries which are used to make jams and, in Portugal, a type of brandy. Traditional herbalists use the leaves for their anti-inflammatory properties as well as for treating urinary infections, rheumatism and diabetes.

Bees enjoy the nectar and frugivorous mammals and birds flock to the fruit.

It is found in countries that surround the Mediterranean; in Spain any fruits that are left on the trees to ripen and ferment are sometimes eaten by bears who become quite tipsy! That might be why the coat of arms for Madrid displays a bear eating the fruit of the strawberry tree.

> a strawberry tree
> a sore head in the morning
> let sleeping bears lie

From the Journal

Nick, our window cleaner came today. It was lovely to see him; it felt as if life is returning infinitely slowly to some sort of normality. We still stood two metres apart for a chat but that's okay. At the same time the postie drew up in his van. He had a parcel for us, a long tube with Dave's glass stringers in, the length of the parcel meant he could hand it over while being safely distant. We laughed at the intrusion into our lives of the Lockdown and social distancing, but it was a good laugh, a healing sort of laugh.

We are lucky to live in a village and our local supermarket is only four miles away. A small catchment area for the shop means we rarely queue to go in or come out. There is a one way system and markings on the floor to ensure you know what a two metre gap looks like!

On the whole people keep to the rules; if we need to pass each other slightly closer than specified we do a sideways shuffle at speed.

I smile and you smile
two trolley widths between us
your t-shirt says 'Hi'

no Bran Flakes again
Lockdown constipation fears
have made them precious

driving to the shop
is my list really complete?
Did I note down – gin?

Lawson Cypress aka Port Orford Cedar
(*Chamaecyparis lawsoniana*)

This tree has rot resistant wood and is used for coffins and shrines in Japan. Some people think the foliage, when crushed, smells like parsley and its timber is reported to have an aroma reminiscent of ginger. Birds like to nest in it to take advantage of the shelter afforded by its leaves when other trees are still only in bud.

The *lawsoniana* part of its name is after the nineteenth-century Scottish plantsman Charles Lawson. It is a native of California and Oregon and was introduced into Britain in 1884 when the seeds were planted in the Lawson Nursery in Edinburgh.

Being in the genus *Chamaecyparis* rather than *Cupressus* is a clue that this is actually known as a 'false' cypress.

It is susceptible to phytophthora fungal diseases thought to be spread by the tyres of vehicles such as logging trucks and off-road vehicles.

> the scent of the wood
> competes with fragrant blossoms
> as the people mourn

Holford Pine
(*Pinus x holfordiana*)

This hybrid of the Mexican white pine (*Pinus ayacahuite*) and the Bhutan pine (*Pinus wallichiana*) arose at Westonbirt Arboretum in 1904 and is named for Sir George Holford who was the owner at the time. The Arboretum is the result of the interest the wealthy Holford family took in trees and shrubs from around the world. I believe the hybridisation initially took place spontaneously but has since been recreated by growers.

It is a large tree with a scaly bark and its leaves are in bundles of five long silvery green needles that droop. The banana shaped pale brown pendulous cones are up to 30 cm long.

It is a fast growing tree with 20 inches or more added each year, so probably not one for the average garden.

> cross pollination
> or grafting on to root stock
> design your own tree

Handkerchief Tree aka Dove or Ghost Tree
(*Davidia involucrata*)

Native to southwest China this tree is easily recognisable when in flower. The white bracts that surround the flower head hang on the tree like pocket hankies or tiny ghosts. It is well named.

The French missionary and botanist, Abbé Armand David, first recorded the tree in 1869 but it was not introduced to Britain until 1901 courtesy of the plant hunter Ernest Henry 'Chinese' Wilson, one of the twenty two or so plant hunters who worked for the Veitch Nursery. Wilson's mission was to find the single tree earlier spotted by another plant hunter Augustin Henry but arrived at the place only to find that it had been cut down to be used for building. He continued to search and eventually found a grove of the trees. During his voyage home he was shipwrecked but managed to save his precious *Davidia* specimens.

The alternative name, the dove tree, has a sad story woven around it. A homesick young woman married off to a 'barbarian' in order to cement an agreement between rulers, sent doves home to her family with messages as she travelled. On arrival they would roost in a tree in the family's garden. The distance the birds had to travel grew with each passing day and the very last dove, which had to fly a thousand miles, died on arrival.

> doves or tiny ghosts
> messengers of such sadness
> flutter in the breeze

Handkerchief tree

Ginkgo biloba

Herbs

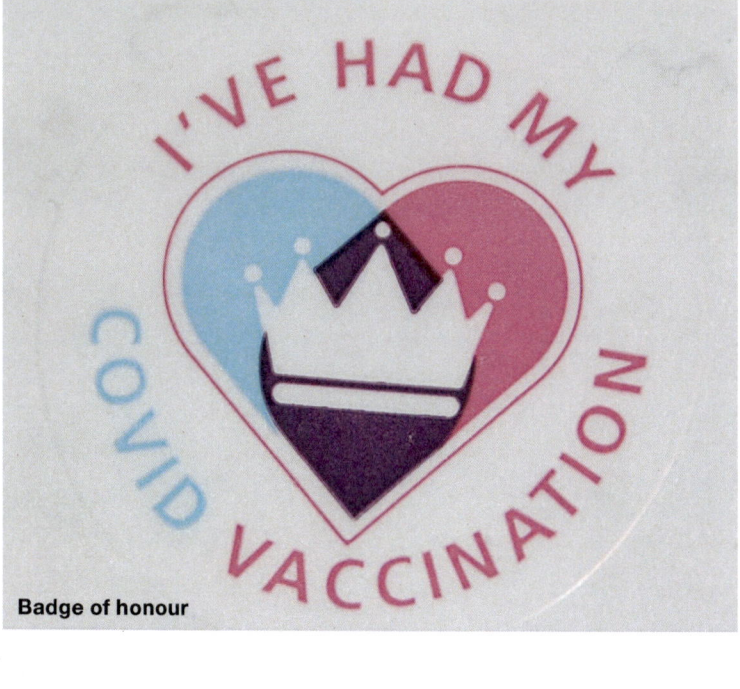

Badge of honour

Furin-tsutsuji
(*Enkianthus campanulatus*)

Often called red-veined enkianthus, this has tiny bell-like flowers that are cream with pink stripes. More of a shrub than a tree, it can grow to 15 feet and is a native of Japan. It was brought to Britain by another of the Veitch plant hunters, Charles Maries.

The strangest fact I found about this plant is that it grows with many other trees and shrubs in a place called Aokigahara, the Sea of Trees, on the flanks of Mount Fuji. The forest was known historically as a haunted place and in recent times has become notorious as one of the most used suicide sites in the world. In the official Aokigahara website I read: 'An annual body sweep is organized before the holiday season in which the found dead bodies are removed and, where possible, identified'.

On a lighter note, *Enkianthus campanulatus* 'Red Bells' holds the Royal Horticultural Society's Award of Garden Merit, which is their seal of approval for a plant that performs reliably when planted in a garden.

>strange – the things you learn
>unlooked for tales of sadness
>burden the flowers

Broad Leaf Lilac
(*Syringa oblate*)

Syringa comes from *syrinx*, the Greek for 'pipe' or 'tube' and refers to the use of the hollow stems to make flutes. A story goes that the Greek nymph Syrinx, who was known for her chastity, ran to the river nymphs to beg for help when she was being pursued by Pan. They helped her by turning her into hollow reeds which made a haunting sound when his breath crossed them. He cut the reeds and hey presto, created Pan pipes. I'm not sure that was what Syrinx had in mind when she cried for help.

The trees flower early and produce showy, fragrant flowers that attract butterflies and people alike.

>something cyclical
>in stories of oppression
>that haunt names of trees

Indian Bean Tree
(*Catalpa bignoniodes*)

This tree is not from India nor does it grow beans, although its seed pods resemble long bean pods, it is native to the south east states of the USA. The bright green heart-shaped leaves and white flowers make it a popular ornamental tree for parks and gardens.

The roots are highly poisonous and I have read conflicting information on how the rest of the tree has been used in alternative medicine for conditions from malaria to asthma to trachoma. So, once again, I would recommend that you take expert advice – not just something that appears on the Internet – if you wish to use any leaves, bark, pods or seeds medicinally.

Its fruit looks like long, thin bean pods and have been known to stay on the trees throughout the winter.

> life and death is found
> all around us – the secret
> is ancient knowledge

Great White Cherry
(*Prunus serrulata* 'Tai-haku')

'The cherry is first among flowers as the samurai is among men'

(Japanese proverb)

Japan opened to Westerners in 1863 and the country was a revelation to travellers. Initially there were around ten native species but with cross pollination and grafting this number grew to 250.

The great white cherry has flowers that are twice the size of other flowering cherries and its bronze red leaves in the spring contrast beautifully with these white blooms to make this a very striking sight.

A man called Collingwood Ingram was fascinated by cherry trees, so much so that he is known as 'Cherry' Ingram! In 1925 a Japanese cherry grower visited Ingram's garden in Kent and was so impressed by his white flowering specimen he named it 'tai-haku' meaning 'big white'.

Then, in 1926, Ingram visited Japan and was shown a scroll that had been illustrated in the 1830s and his host pointed to a picture of their finest flowering tree and told him that it had died out years before. Ingram looked at it and told them that it was still growing in his own garden in England. He then decided to try to reintroduce it to Japan and came up with the idea of poking the cuttings into potatoes to keep them damp. He sent them on a railway journey across Russia to Japan ensuring they remained cool, rather than sending them on a sea journey via tropical parts. The result? *Prunus* 'tai-haku' now grows and flowers once more in Japan.

the great white cherry
each brief glimpse comforts us now
that not all is lost

Postscript

Nothing has brought home to us more vividly that we are part of a huge community than these past years. We have seen heroism in the smallest of acts as well as the lifesaving work of our National Health Service. Scientists have come to the fore as we learn about their painstaking work creating and developing means by which we can fight back against Covid; massive efforts have been made by nurses, doctors and volunteers to mass vaccinate the population against this new virus. Teachers have had to find ways of teaching their students in the virtual world; delivery drivers have become part of the emergency response; recycling collectors, shop assistants and a host of others have, at last, been recognised as the people we all depend on in a crisis. We owe them a huge debt of thanks.

Get out there, enjoy the world wherever you live and, as we look to the future, I wish you all good health and happiness!

Bibliography

Sterry, P. *Collins Complete Guide to British Trees.* (2007) London: HarperCollins Publisher Ltd.
Arnoldia, https://arboretum.harvard.edu/arnoldia/
Natural Resources Wales, https://naturalresources.wales/
Trees for Life, https://treesforlife.org.uk/
Discover Wildlife, www.discoverwildlife.com
Forestry England, www.forestryengland.uk
Kew Gardens, www.kew.org
Royal Horticultural Society, www.rhs.org.uk
Plant Explorers, www.plantexplorers.com
Woodland Trust, www.woodlandtrust.org.uk